The Power of I Am

Katrina M. Henderson

Published by Katrina M. Henderson

Editing and graphic design by Karen Bowlding

Cover image by Midjourney (AI)

ISBN 979-8-9894971-0-2

-Hey Beautiful-

This moment is all about YOU. The YOU ready to create something beautiful. Within the depths of you lies an incredible beautiful force waiting to be unleashed. It's a power that can transform your life, shape your destiny, and inspire you to reach your authentic self. This is the "Power of I Am," which holds the key to unlocking your beautiful (your true potential).

You may often find yourself struggling with self-doubt, societies expectations, and other pressures to conform to a limited definition of beautiful. And because of this, you may forget the remarkable strength, resilience, and confidence that lives within you.

On this journey, you are going to reflect on who you are when no one is looking! You are going to call in, manifest and tap into what motivates you, challenges you, and pushes you to reach your beautiful life. You WILL re-write the narrative and embrace the truth of who we are.

For 31 days, I want you to find a quiet space and sit down (preferably first thing in the morning) when the house is still sleep. Read the daily devotion and affirmation. Repeat the affirmation three times a day and reflect on your beautiful life you are creating. Allow the words to unleash the beautiful within you! I'm excited for the beauty that will be revealed as you discover the "Power of I Am."

~ Katrina

Day 1

I am ALL I am called to be!

Hey Beautiful! Within you lies an extraordinary power waiting to acknowledge and embrace. You possess the strength, resilience, and wisdom to make yourself powerful. Begin the beautiful journey of self-acceptance and self-love as you accept and honor who you as your true power emerges.

Recognize the growth you have achieved and celebrate your accomplishments, big and small. Embrace your strengths and flaws and know that they are all part of the beautiful composition that makes you the beautiful woman you are. Embrace your beautiful uniqueness, talents, and passions, for they are the key to unleashing your fullest potential. Embrace the power that comes from fully knowing and accepting yourself, and let it guide you towards a life filled with purpose, joy, and abundance. Today, believe in the all you have been called to be.

-Journaling Reflection-

What extraordinary power lives within you? What is God calling you to do?

_____

_____

_____

_____

_____

_____

_____

_____

_____

_____

_____

_____

_____

_____

_____

_____

_____

_____

_____

_____

_____

_____

_____

Day 2

I have all the power to create the beautiful life I desire!

Hey Beautiful! Today is all about reclaiming you! It's the time to reflect on who you are when no one is looking! This is key because too many of us often wear a mask. We don't let the real person out because we don't want to be hurt. We don't want anyone to know who we are for the fear that they may not like the real us. Now is the time to manifest the power of YOU by shifting your mindset!

Today, create the beautiful life you want! You have the power to call in what you desire because God gives you that desire. He's going to give you the steps needed to manifest it. You have to believe what's possible and be open and available to create what you desire!

-Journaling Reflection-

What beautiful life do you have the desire to create?

_____

_____

_____

_____

_____

_____

_____

_____

_____

_____

_____

_____

_____

_____

_____

_____

_____

_____

_____

_____

_____

_____

_____

_____

_____

Day 3

I am equipped for everything that comes my way!

Hey Beautiful! No matter what you're going through and what's taking place, you are equipped for every single thing happening! Continue to stand your ground. Continue to stand in your beautiful. Continue to push because He is with you every step of the way. God has you. You are equipped for everything that's coming your way! After all, this is the beauty of the journey: knowing you are never alone.

-Journaling Reflection-

Reflect on your past challenges and how you overcame them. What did you learn from those beautiful experiences that have prepared you for this very moment?

_____

_____

_____

_____

_____

_____

_____

_____

_____

_____

_____

_____

_____

_____

_____

_____

_____

_____

_____

_____

Day 4

I have enough. I do enough. I am enough!

Hey Beautiful! You have enough! You do enough! You are enough! Everything you have is enough! You want more but shift your thinking, your thoughts and your belief system to that of gratitude. Be grateful for what you have instead of always wanting more. Be grateful for THIS moment!

Reassess all that you do. Take a look at your to-do list and complete what you can. Don't stress about what doesn't get done. Perhaps, that task wasn't intended for you to complete because you took on someone else's assignment! Know that you are enough, so much so, that everything you desire and want to manifest are yours. You are worthy and equipped to have it all!

-Journaling Reflection-

What limiting beliefs do you need to release to receive that you are enough?

_____

_____

_____

_____

_____

_____

_____

_____

_____

_____

_____

_____

_____

_____

_____

_____

_____

_____

_____

_____

_____

_____

_____

_____

Day 5

What I have in my hands right NOW is more important than what I am waiting to have!

Hey Beautiful! Focus on and appreciate what you have right now! No longer take the moment for granted. Appreciate your NOW in hopes of and in anticipation of the things to come. Many of us want to change some things or do things differently in our lives based on what we learned. Because of our steps or missteps, we are here at this very moment. Appreciate everything—the good, the bad, the ugly, the tears, and the smiles! Get ready to go into your next!

Be grateful for what you have right now! Love what you have right NOW! Look at your beautiful life and say, "God, I thank you!"

-Journaling Reflection-

What are you grateful for right NOW in this beautiful moment?

_____

_____

_____

_____

_____

_____

_____

_____

_____

_____

_____

_____

_____

_____

_____

_____

_____

_____

_____

_____

_____

_____

Day 6

I am more amazing minute by minute!

Hey Beautiful! Today is all about celebrating you and how amazing you are! Toot your own horn and celebrate you by reminding yourself that you are amazing second by second, minute by minute, hour by hour, day by day, year by year! You are absolutely amazing! Understand, believe, and remember this when you are going through the trials, when somebody comes at you talking crazy and insane, and you're having this "is this really happening moment." Remember, you are amazing minute by minute.

Stop waiting for someone to celebrate you. Take action to inspire your own beautiful. Take your power back and celebrate you every day regardless of whether someone is celebrating with you. You are absolutely amazing! You are absolutely beautiful! You are absolutely confident, worthy, equipped, called, and whole. You are all of it and more!

-Journaling Reflection-

What changes have you noticed within yourself that have made you the amazingly beautiful women you are today?

_____

_____

_____

_____

_____

_____

_____

_____

_____

_____

_____

_____

_____

_____

_____

_____

_____

_____

_____

_____

_____

_____

Day 7

I am meant to be here at this beautiful moment!

Hey Beautiful! This is the season of trusting and believing in manifesting what you desire. When you say "yes," there's nothing that you can't do. God is going to give you what you need when you need it. It may not seem like it when you first hear it, but He will give you what you need. Remind yourself that you are meant for THIS beautiful moment. No more shrinking. No more wondering if God gave you the assignment.

He gave you today. He said, "This is it." Be grateful. Encourage yourself. Nothing is too small. Nothing is too big. If God gave it to you, He's going to help you walk that thing out.

-Journaling Reflection-

What are you trusting and believing God for in this beautiful moment?

_____

_____

_____

_____

_____

_____

_____

_____

_____

_____

_____

_____

_____

_____

_____

_____

_____

_____

_____

_____

_____

_____

_____

_____

-*Weekly Reflection*-

Hey Beautiful! You have completed a week discovering *The Power of I Am*. Write your reflections and set your intentions for the week to come. What beautiful moments have you experienced in this past week?

_____

_____

_____

_____

_____

_____

_____

_____

_____

_____

_____

_____

_____

_____

_____

_____

_____

_____

_____

_____

_____

_____

What intentions are you setting for the upcoming week?

_____

_____

_____

_____

_____

_____

_____

_____

_____

_____

_____

_____

_____

_____

_____

_____

_____

_____

_____

_____

_____

_____

_____

_____

_____

_____

_____

_____

What beliefs or fears do you need to release prior to going into the upcoming week?

_____

_____

_____

_____

_____

_____

_____

_____

_____

_____

_____

_____

_____

_____

_____

_____

_____

_____

_____

_____

_____

_____

_____

_____

_____

Day 8

I am who I need to be today!

Hey Beautiful! In your journey to beautiful, you have a unique path to discovering your true self. Allow yourself the freedom to grow and evolve at your own pace. This way, you become present in your beautiful moments, which allows you the opportunity to blossom into who you were created to be.

You are exactly where you need to be at this moment. It's about progress not perfection. Avoid comparing yourself to others because you don't know their journey. Embrace your worth and the rest will follow!

-Journaling Reflection-

Reflect on what's kept you from moving forward. What or who do you need to release TODAY?

_____
_____
_____
_____
_____
_____
_____
_____
_____
_____
_____
_____
_____
_____
_____
_____
_____
_____
_____
_____
_____
_____

Day 9

I walk in the confidence of
who I have been created to be!

Hey Beautiful! Continue walking in the confidence of who you have been created to be! When things don't go the way you want, you may get thrown off course and your fears may take hold. When the steps you need to take aren't clear, you may get distracted. Whatever it is, you must be able to say, "No matter what's coming at me, no matter what missing pieces I don't have, I'm going to continue to walk in this thing with confidence." This is what the journey of trusting God for your beautiful is about. It's letting Him know to sustain you so that you can walk and step out your beautiful.

-Journaling Reflection-

Reflect on your strengths, talents, and beautiful. What hinders you from believing in the confidence of who God created you to be?

_____

_____

_____

_____

_____

_____

_____

_____

_____

_____

_____

_____

_____

_____

_____

_____

_____

_____

_____

_____

_____

_____

_____

Day 10

I have the abundance I desire!

Hey Beautiful! Are you creating? Are you believing in what you pray for? Are you living for the abundance you desire? Part of being able to manifest something is believing in it. Believe that you are worthy enough. Believe that it's available to you. Believe that it's yours. You can have the abundance you desire but you have to ask for it. You've got to believe it. You've got to reach for it. You've got to work for it. You've got to do whatever you need to be able to attract it. Activate your faith. Activate and take action. You have the ability to create the abundance you desire.

-Journaling Reflection-

What do you want to create in the beautiful life you desire?
What's preventing you from believing for it?

_____

_____

_____

_____

_____

_____

_____

_____

_____

_____

_____

_____

_____

_____

_____

_____

_____

_____

_____

_____

_____

_____

_____

_____

Day 11

I am content with who I am created to be!

Hey Beautiful! Be aware of who you are. Be aware of who you have been created to be. Be aware of what you are to do. Stop looking at what you should have done. Have no regrets or doubts or fears. You are not as far from where you think you should be. In God's timing, you are exactly where you should be. You are exactly who you are to be.

Be content with where you are. Stop saying, "Woe is me." Stop saying the shoulda coulda woulda. Be grateful for this very beautiful moment. Be at peace with who you have been created to be.

-Journaling Reflection-

Who are you when you believe in yourself? Who are you when no one is watching?

_____

_____

_____

_____

_____

_____

_____

_____

_____

_____

_____

_____

_____

_____

_____

_____

_____

_____

_____

_____

_____

Day 12

Every experience I have is perfect for my growth!

Hey Beautiful! No matter how much you want to change your circumstances, there are certain things you have no control over. Despite how much you plan ahead, things are going to happen. Rather than looking at your circumstances as a stumbling block, see them as opportunities for your growth. See the lesson in everything you encounter.

Make no mistake, you can get through this because you've made it through worse. Keep believing and pushing. You are a conqueror! Every experience you have is perfect to further your growth!

-Journaling Reflection-

Reflect on your past challenges and control you tried to have. What do you need to surrender?

_____

_____

_____

_____

_____

_____

_____

_____

_____

_____

_____

_____

_____

_____

_____

_____

_____

_____

_____

_____

_____

_____

Day 13

I am at peace when I follow my intuition!

Hey Beautiful! Be at peace and trust your instinct. Maybe your instinct is telling you to have a hard conversation, you need to let a relationship go, or you should start the business. It's time to get out of your pity party and believe in your beautiful.

You have to release whatever you've been holding. You must allow your intuition to be heard. It can't be heard if you don't forgive. It can't be heard if you don't live your beautiful life. You are worth so much more than your situation. Whether you are divorced, missing love from your father, have hurt feelings, or disappointed you didn't get promotion, whatever your "it" is, you are worth more than your it. The only way you're going to find peace is by following your intuition and letting go of the pain.

-Journaling Reflection-

Reflect on your past challenges. What is your intuition telling you to do? What is pulling on your heart at this very moment?

_____

_____

_____

_____

_____

_____

_____

_____

_____

_____

_____

_____

_____

_____

_____

_____

_____

_____

_____

_____

_____

_____

Day 14

I deserve this life!

Hey Beautiful! Repeat, "I deserve this life!" Sit in the power of these words. You can create the life you want because it's a matter of believing you have the power to create the life you deserve. Believe in what's possible. Believe in the magic of who you are.

Circumstance tries to dictate that you don't deserve the life that you want. It tries to tell you that your pain will never allow you to be anything other than pain. It tries to tell you that you can never have a better life. Well Beautiful, this is far from the truth. You can have everything you desire because you deserve it. You don't have to perform to get it. Just be you! Today, acknowledge that you deserve this life!

-Journaling Reflection-

Reflect on the lies you have told to yourself, or others have told to you. What do you need to acknowledge to say, "I deserve this life?"

_____

_____

_____

_____

_____

_____

_____

_____

_____

_____

_____

_____

_____

_____

_____

_____

_____

_____

_____

_____

_____

-Weekly Reflection-

Hey Beautiful! You have completed a week discovering *The Power of I Am*. Write your reflections and set your intentions for the week to come. What beautiful moments have you experienced in this past week?

_____

_____

_____

_____

_____

_____

_____

_____

_____

_____

_____

_____

_____

_____

_____

_____

_____

_____

_____

_____

_____

_____

_____

_____

What intentions are you setting for the upcoming week?

_____

_____

_____

_____

_____

_____

_____

_____

_____

_____

_____

_____

_____

_____

_____

_____

_____

_____

_____

_____

_____

_____

_____

_____

_____

What beliefs or fears do you need to release prior to going into the upcoming week?

_____

_____

_____

_____

_____

_____

_____

_____

_____

_____

_____

_____

_____

_____

_____

_____

_____

_____

_____

_____

_____

_____

_____

_____

_____

Day 15

I believe in the magic of who I am!

Hey Beautiful! Don't let anyone or any situation dull your shine. You are magic! You can create everything you desire. Stand your ground for what you want. Don't let anyone convince you of something you don't want because of their fears. Don't sacrifice what you want because you don't want to disappoint someone by saying, "No." Trust me, they will get over it. If you are claiming your beautiful then there's magic in every situation! Honor what you want.

Honor what you create. Believe in your beautiful, what you bring to the table, exude, and the magic you create. You have the power and the magic to create everything, and I mean everything you want.

-Journaling Reflection-

Close your eyes and see the magic of who you are. Describe the magic of who you are. What do you want?

_____

_____

_____

_____

_____

_____

_____

_____

_____

_____

_____

_____

_____

_____

_____

_____

_____

_____

_____

_____

_____

_____

Day 16

Today is my NOW! I will live in this beautiful moment!

Hey Beautiful! Believe, understand, and accept that this beautiful moment is what it's all about. With everything you've experienced—the fears, failures, mistakes, blessings, manifestations, everything is a part of right now. It is a part of this beautiful moment, so continue to live. Stop doubting, stop questioning, start being more open, and start receiving!

This is your receiving season so be open to receiving. Invite the blessings in by believing in this beautiful moment. Today, change your mindset by saying, "I allow, I accept, and I receive this beautiful moment." You don't have to worry about tomorrow or yesterday because you are present in your now.

-Journaling Reflection-

What do you need to allow, accept, and receive?

_____

_____

_____

_____

_____

_____

_____

_____

_____

_____

_____

_____

_____

_____

_____

_____

_____

_____

_____

_____

_____

_____

_____

Day 17

I am ready to love myself just as I am!

Hey Beautiful! No one can change everything about themselves. If you have something you want to change, but couldn't, would you be okay with it? Can you be okay with loving yourself just as you are? Most of us want to change some things such as losing weight, fixing an attitude issue, or having more money in the bank. But can you be fine if nothing changed?

Be grateful for where you currently are because it could be worse. Look at everything you have gone through and overcome and appreciate where you are! Appreciate who you are! Appreciate where you are! Appreciate, honor, acknowledge, and accept who you are at this very moment!

-Journaling Reflection-

Can you be okay with who you currently are? If not, what do you need to do to change your view?

_____

_____

_____

_____

_____

_____

_____

_____

_____

_____

_____

_____

_____

_____

_____

_____

_____

_____

_____

_____

_____

_____

_____

Day 18

No approval is needed for me
to live this beautiful life!

Hey Beautiful! No approval is needed for you to live this beautiful life. Sometimes, you may do something with hesitation because you might be looking for someone's approval. Start trusting in yourself. Start trusting in your intuition. Start believing in your greater. No approval is needed for you to live your beautiful life. You are equipped and called for your beautiful life!

-Journaling Reflection-

Reflect on your need for approval. What must you tell yourself so that you will no longer look for it?

_____
_____
_____
_____
_____
_____
_____
_____
_____
_____
_____
_____
_____
_____
_____
_____
_____
_____
_____
_____
_____
_____
_____
_____
_____

Day 19

I am divine and called to my purpose!

Hey Beautiful! You are divine and called to purpose. And this means no matter what you go through or what obstacles come your way, nothing can change that you've been called for more. The obstacles, trials, roadblocks, detours you've had to make...none of those matters. None of that hinders the call and purpose you have on your life.

You are divine and called to purpose. Keep saying it over and over! Write it! Speak it out loud! Do whatever you have to do to remember this. Know that the next time your trial hits and you wonder what's happening, you'll know you're called to purpose. It's in that moment you realize this is just part of the beautiful journey. As such, nothing is going to change the final outcome because your destiny will be manifested regardless of what it looks like right now. Did you hear me? You are divine and called to purpose.

-Journaling Reflection-

What purpose have you been called to? What steps can you take to walk in your purpose?

_____

_____

_____

_____

_____

_____

_____

_____

_____

_____

_____

_____

_____

_____

_____

_____

_____

_____

_____

_____

_____

_____

_____

Day 20

I can and will change my beautiful life!

Hey Beautiful! The beautiful thing about this journey is that no matter what you go through, all of it is a part of the process. It may not seem like it when you're going through it, but it is. You're probably thinking, "Why would God allow me to go through this?" I'd ask the question, "Why wouldn't He let you go through this?" Consider the lessons you received, the choices you made, and the reliance and trust you had in Him as you're going through different circumstances.

Look at your circumstances differently from what you have been accustomed to. Through your circumstances, you've built resilience, strength, courage, and confidence. Today, reflect on what you need to accept, receive, and release to create the beautiful life you undeniably deserve!

-Journaling Reflection-

Reflect on your past challenges. What do you need to accept to create the beautiful life you deserve?

_____

_____

_____

_____

_____

_____

_____

_____

_____

_____

_____

_____

_____

_____

_____

_____

_____

_____

_____

_____

_____

_____

_____

Day 21

I fully embrace who I am!

Hey Beautiful! The *you* that you see is all you need to be. Embrace who you are. Accept the good, the bad and the ugly. Embrace it all! Everything about you is beautiful. Everything about you is perfect. Everything about you is unique. Embrace everything about you—the things you love, the things you wish you could change, and all of the shoulda coulda woulda's. Embrace all of this because it's all of you!

God has created you to be just as you are. He knew you were going to fall short, have challenges, and self-doubt. He knew all of that because He *is* the answer to all of that. Welcome and receive all of who you are. You are the beautiful soul that you have been created to be.

-Journaling Reflection-

What does the little girl inside of you need to hear to embrace all of who she is?

_____

_____

_____

_____

_____

_____

_____

_____

_____

_____

_____

_____

_____

_____

_____

_____

_____

_____

_____

_____

_____

_____

-*Weekly Reflection*-

Hey Beautiful! You have completed a week discovering *The Power of I Am*. Write your reflections and set the intentions for the week to come. What beautiful moments have you experienced in this past week?

_____

_____

_____

_____

_____

_____

_____

_____

_____

_____

_____

_____

_____

_____

_____

_____

_____

_____

_____

_____

_____

_____

What intentions are you setting for the upcoming week?

_____
_____
_____
_____
_____
_____
_____
_____
_____
_____
_____
_____
_____
_____
_____
_____
_____
_____
_____
_____
_____
_____
_____
_____
_____
_____
_____

What beliefs or fears do you need to release prior to going into the upcoming week?

_____

_____

_____

_____

_____

_____

_____

_____

_____

_____

_____

_____

_____

_____

_____

_____

_____

_____

_____

_____

_____

_____

_____

_____

_____

Day 22

In everything I do, I lead with love!

Hey Beautiful! Within you resides a beautiful power that can transform your life! Allow your power to recognize that love is not only a beautiful force that connects but also flows within you. When you lead with love, you cultivate self-acceptance and self-love, paving the way for your confidence to blossom.

Embrace the truth that you are deserving of love, kindness, and compassion. In nurturing your own well-being and embracing your beautiful, you will radiate a magnetic energy that inspires others and creates a beautiful ripple effect. In other words, you are creating your beauty mark. Embrace your power to create and choose love to make an impact on the world. Your actions, no matter how small, can create a ripple of beautiful that extends far beyond what you can imagine. Embrace the power of leading with love, and watch as it unlocks your true beautiful, bringing fulfillment, joy, and harmonious connections into your life.

-Journaling Reflection-

What beauty mark do you have to share with the world?

_____

_____

_____

_____

_____

_____

_____

_____

_____

_____

_____

_____

_____

_____

_____

_____

_____

_____

_____

_____

_____

_____

_____

Day 23

I am open to receive the abundance waiting for me!

Hey Beautiful! Receiving is a hard thing when you're a giver, right? You're always giving, but this is the time to receive, to be open and do what's necessary. Are you open for what you're asking from God? You can't just believe for what you are asking for, you must be open to receive it.

Be open to be in the process of peeling back all of your layers. Dig out of the hurt, pain, and shame! Any discomfort you may feel is putting you in a position to be open for everything you've desired, called into your life, and want to manifest. It's not easy to put yourself in a position to receive when you're so used to giving to others. Now is your time to be the recipient of every beautiful thing life has to offer because you are deserving and worthy.

-Journaling Reflection-

What beautiful things are waiting for you to say, "Yes?"
What beautiful things are waiting for you to receive?

_____
_____
_____
_____
_____
_____
_____
_____
_____
_____
_____
_____
_____
_____
_____
_____
_____
_____
_____
_____
_____
_____
_____

Day 24

I am capable of more than I think!

Hey Beautiful! Some of us may think that because we go through trials or don't have enough money or talent that we can't complete our assignment. When you feel this way, it's the moment to trust God to give you what you need. So today, don't think about what you can't do. Believe what you are capable of doing because you are equipped and called for this very moment. You don't have to have it all together to move forward. You don't have to have all the steps laid out for you to work on a goal. You don't have to have everything wrapped up in a pretty bow to move in the assignment or into your calling. It's just a matter of taking a step!

Today, as you go about your day, honor and appreciate what you are capable of doing, accomplishing, walking into, and living! You are capable of more than you think!

-Journaling Reflection-

Reflect on how far you've come and the assignment you were given. What steps do you need to take to accomplish your greatest desire?

_____

_____

_____

_____

_____

_____

_____

_____

_____

_____

_____

_____

_____

_____

_____

_____

_____

_____

_____

_____

_____

_____

Day 25

I know I am called!

Hey Beautiful! You are called to purpose. You are called to more. You are called to bigger things. You are called to manifest what it is you desire. You are called! Walk in your power! Release your fears, doubts, and procrastination. Release the notion and let go of the belief that you lack the necessary tools or resources to pursue your dreams. You don't need all the technology or a perfect plan.

Break free from what keeps you stuck or complacent. Your genius lies outside of your comfort zone. Step out and don't settle for comfort. Push yourself and learn new things. You are called, and you have what it takes. Embrace the journey and welcome the evolution of your beautiful!

-Journaling Reflection-

What fears, doubts, and procrastination do you need to release to believe that you are called?

_____

_____

_____

_____

_____

_____

_____

_____

_____

_____

_____

_____

_____

_____

_____

_____

_____

_____

_____

_____

_____

_____

_____

_____

Day 26

I am proud of who I am!

Hey Beautiful! Acknowledge the beautiful work you've been doing! It's time to celebrate and be proud of who you are. Embrace the beautiful journey you're on! On your journey, you will experience all kinds of beautiful moments—triumphs and challenges, which make up who you are. Be grateful for what you've experienced along your beautiful journey.

Understand that though every beautiful experience, whether joyful or painful, you have been shaped into the beautiful woman you are. Recognize your ability to create the beautiful life you desire. Take a moment to appreciate how far you've come. You overcame challenges that once seemed impossible. Honor and celebrate yourself as you take pride in how far you've come!

-Journaling Reflection-

Reflect on your beautiful journey. What should you celebrate about yourself?

_____

_____

_____

_____

_____

_____

_____

_____

_____

_____

_____

_____

_____

_____

_____

_____

_____

_____

_____

_____

_____

_____

_____

Day 27

Wisdom and truth flow through me with ease!

Hey Beautiful! Within you lies a depth of wisdom and truth waiting to be recognized and embraced. In your beautiful journey, understand that you possess the power to illuminate your beautiful path and inspire others. Trust in your intuition and the knowledge that resides within you. Embrace the power of your beautiful experiences, both the triumphs and the challenges, for they have shaped you into who you are today.

Recognize that you have the ability to navigate life's complexities with grace, clarity, and ease. Embrace your inner voice and let it guide you towards making choices aligned with your beautiful values and desires. Embrace the strength of your beautiful and the authenticity of your being. As you tap into your wisdom and speak your truth, you empower yourself by creating a ripple of beautiful in the world. Embrace the power of your inner beauty and let it flow through you with ease!

-Journaling Reflection-

What beautiful light within you needs to be illuminated for others to see?

_____

_____

_____

_____

_____

_____

_____

_____

_____

_____

_____

_____

_____

_____

_____

_____

_____

_____

_____

_____

_____

_____

Day 28

I am unstoppable and can accomplish everything I try!

Hey Beautiful! The key to manifesting what you want is taking the first step. You've got to put in some effort to obtain the beautiful you desire. It's one thing to have the faith. It's another to move forward in faith! You can have the faith, but you must do your part. To be in alignment, you have to slow down and be still enough to hear. You can't have so much chaos around and in you or you will miss the steps to be taken.

Today, take the time to sit, be still, and process what it is you want to accomplish. Allow Heaven to speak. You can accomplish whatever you desire because you are unstoppable.

-Journaling Reflection-

What action steps do you need to take to believe you are unstoppable?

_____
_____
_____
_____
_____
_____
_____
_____
_____
_____
_____
_____
_____
_____
_____
_____
_____
_____
_____
_____

Day 29

I am capable of creating a beautiful life!

Hey Beautiful! The power to create a beautiful life is in your hands. God has created the power within you, but you have to realize and understand that you are worthy of having it all. Embrace the beautiful power within you to create a life of beauty, fulfillment, and purpose. You possess the creativity, resilience, and strength to shape your own beautiful destiny. Embrace your gifts, talents, and passions, for they are the building blocks of the beautiful life you envision.

Embrace the power of your thoughts, intentions, and actions to create the life you desire. Trust in your beautiful, and let it guide you towards making empowered choices. Embrace your worthiness, deservingness of all the beauty and abundance that life has to offer. As you align with your true power, you become the "beautiful" for others to see! You show what's possible because you've created your beautiful life!

-Journaling Reflection-

What thoughts, intentions, or actions must you embrace to create your beautiful life?

_____

_____

_____

_____

_____

_____

_____

_____

_____

_____

_____

_____

_____

_____

_____

_____

_____

_____

_____

_____

_____

_____

_____

Day 30

Today is the future I created yesterday!

Hey Beautiful! Everything that happened years, months, weeks, minutes or even seconds ago, prepared you for this very moment! Without challenges and missteps, you wouldn't be who you are today. You wouldn't be pushing as hard as you do! You wouldn't be creating and accomplishing goals! You wouldn't leave the beauty marks that we get to experience in this world! And this is because your past created your future, and we are grateful!

-Journaling Reflection-

Reflect on how the choices and actions of your past led you to the present moment. How can you create a more fulfilling future by being mindful of your choices today?

_____

_____

_____

_____

_____

_____

_____

_____

_____

_____

_____

_____

_____

_____

_____

_____

_____

_____

_____

_____

Day 31

Today, my life is beautiful!

Hey Beautiful! Your life is beautiful! Know it, believe it, hold onto it, and understand it! On your beautiful journey, you get to experience so much—the creation of everything that you desire, everything you manifested, the beauty marks you left in the world. So, celebrate this! Cherish and honor getting to the finish line of creating your beautiful life!

-Journaling Reflection-

Celebrate the completion of this 31-day affirmation journey. What growth have you experienced? What insights did you gain? What positive changes have you made on your beautiful journey?

_____

_____

_____

_____

_____

_____

_____

_____

_____

_____

_____

_____

_____

_____

_____

_____

_____

_____

_____

_____

_____

Hey Beautiful, Congratulations

Over the course of 31 days, you embarked on a beautiful and transformative journey of self-discovery and empowerment through *The Power of I Am*. Throughout the journey, you learned to recognize and acknowledge your inner power, strength, resilience, and your beautiful. You embraced the idea that you have everything you need to create the beautiful life you desire, and you let go of any feelings of inadequacy, knowing that you are enough just as you are. You shifted your perspective from dwelling on what you lack to appreciating and valuing what you have in the present moment. You celebrated the beauty of the here and now and recognized that this very moment holds infinite possibilities for creating a fulfilling beautiful life.

As you move forward, embrace the lessons you've learned and carry the beautiful empowering mindset with you as you continue to create a beautiful life that aligns with your true purpose. Remember, you have the power within you to embrace the magic of who you are and live a life filled with abundance and fulfillment. Trust in yourself and the journey that lies ahead. You are meant to be here, embracing all the beauty and potential that life has to offer. Keep believing in the beautiful person you are and continue to let your light shine brightly for the world to see. You are beautiful, powerful, and unstoppable! You've created a beautiful life!

~Katrina

About the Author

Katrina M. Henderson is the Chief Beautiful Officer and owner of Unbreakable Memories, which is not just another jewelry, t-shirt, journal, candle, or home decor brand. It's a brand that believes in the power of "Beautiful".

With her Hello My Name is Beautiful® movement, Katrina is inspiring women and girls to define their beautiful. She encourages women to stop looking at their outward beauty and look toward the beauty within them and accept themselves as the beautiful they were created to be! She is encouraging girls to define their beautiful by celebrating what makes them beautiful. She is changing the narrative on beautiful!

Join the Movement

Connect with the movement and share your transformational journey using the hashtag below. Let's inspire each other to embrace our power and beauty within!

Hashtag

#HelloMyNameIsBeautiful

Website

https://www.unbreakablememories.com

Email

katrina@unbreakablememories.com

Social Media

Instagram @hellomynameisbeautiful

YouTube @hellomynameisbeautiful

Facebook @Unbreakablememories

TikTok @hellomynameisbeautiful

www.ingramcontent.com/pod-product-compliance
Lightning Source LLC
Chambersburg PA
CBHW060348130626
46553CB00003B/1134